22-13

# The great funnies
## a history of film comedy

Designed by Gillian Greenwood

David Robinson

# The great funnies

## a history of film comedy

**Studio Vista | Dutton Pictureback**
General editor David Herbert

## Acknowledgments

Special thanks are due to the staff of the Information Department and Stills Library of the National Film Archive.

Stills by courtesy of the Cinémathèque Française, the National Film Archive, Columbia Pictures, Connoisseur Films, Film Polski, London Screenplays, MGM, Paramount, Sovexportfilm, United Artists, Universal Pictures, Warner Brothers, and the author's collection.

© David Robinson 1969
Published in Great Britain by Studio Vista Limited
Blue Star House, Highgate Hill, London N19
and in the United States of America by E. P. Dutton and Co. Inc.
201 Park Avenue South, New York, NY10003
Set in Univers 8 on 11 pt
Made and printed in Great Britain
by Richard Clay (The Chaucer Press) Limited
Bungay, Suffolk

SBN 289 79640 7 (paperback)
    289 79643 1 (hardback)

# Contents

## Preface

It would be impossible in a book of this size to offer anything like a comprehensive survey of the vast, tumbling, chattering, shrieking army of clowns who have peopled the first seventy years of the cinema ; and this essay pretends to be no more than a bird's-eye view, only lingering from time to time over a figure of particular importance or special attraction. Even so, everyone will find some of his favourites forgotten, or written off in an inadequate aside. I can only apologize for the inevitable.

The section of the book devoted to silent comedy may seem disproportionate ; but I have felt it important to give space to the more remote and unfamiliar film comedians than to dwell on artists who are still active or whose work can readily be seen at first hand.

## The beginnings

The cinema arrived at a singularly fortunate moment in entertainment history, when an audience and an art of clowning lay ready for the taking. The new, assertive proletarian societies of the industrial revolution had brought into being a new popular audience; and in Europe and America important traditions of popular theatrical entertainment had grown up in the nineteenth century to meet the needs of that audience. Out of the illegitimate theatres and song cellars and supper rooms and pleasure gardens of the early and mid-century had come the British music hall. In America vaudeville had developed by a comparable process. France had its caff'concerts and its own music hall; and there were native equivalents in Italy, Germany, Scandinavia and Russia.

In all these popular theatres the comic tradition was especially strong. The market for comedy is constant: when life is bad people want to laugh; and when they are happy they want, equally, to enjoy themselves. In consequence comedy flourished on the music halls, and the halls proved a unique training ground for the skills of its practitioners. Competition was severe and audiences were demanding and critical. To survive, the music hall or vaudeville comedian had to learn to put over his act in the brief time allotted to him on the bill, to win over an audience against the rival attractions of twenty other acts and the bar at the back of the theatre, to harness the energy and applause and laughter of that audience to provide a springboard to his comedy. The audience seemed not to mind how often it saw a good act; and touring the music hall circuits a comedian could refine and sharpen his business over many years and many performances. W. C. Fields' juggling, Gus Elen's songs, Little Tich's eccentric dancing and patter, Harry Tate's sketches were perfected through years of trial against every kind of audience. Thus, when the cinema made its appearance in the mid-nineties, there was a richer tradition of popular theatrical comedy than, perhaps, at any other period in the history of entertainment.

But if the cinema was fortunate to find a ready-made audience and tradition of comedy, the clowns were fortunate to find the cinema. The comedian had never had such an arena as moving pictures were eventually to offer him. He had now the whole real world out of which to make his comedy. No longer need he be content with painted sets and pasteboard props. He could fall into real lakes, crash real cars, rob real shops, fall off real horses, flee from policemen through real streets and roads and forests.

Nor need he now scale up his playing to reach the back of the gallery. The cinema screen showed him larger than life; the close-up would later enable him to refine his comedy to a detail and subtlety hitherto impossible. The cinema offered new opportunities for comic magic. Suddenly the clown was released from everyday notions of time and space and logic. He could make life move faster or slower, make objects—or even himself—appear and vanish at will. He could appear to walk on the ceiling, or fall off skyscrapers, or disintegrate his body and limbs. It was a world which clowns had always dreamed of, in which physical laws were all subject to the rule of laughter.

None of this was at first apparent. It is hard today to understand how long it was before the first film-makers realized that the cinema could be a theatrical or entertainment art; or indeed any-thing more than a scientific toy of limited interest and temporary profit. The earliest films, running for barely a minute, were regarded only as moving photographs; and the most popular subjects—high seas, arrival of a train, street scenes and so on— would have been equally appropriate to static lantern slides or picture postcards.

Thus, associating the film with *pictures* rather than the theatre or real life, film-makers turned for their comic themes to an existing tradition of static and pictorial humour. Out of the nineteenth-century taste for story-pictures had naturally arisen a style of comic anecdotal drawing. *Punch* had adapted and sophisticated a pictorial humour which itself derived from eighteenth- and early nineteenth-century broadside caricaturists. Stereoscope slides, magic lantern pictures and later the comic picture postcard had adapted photography to the same mode of graphic humour.

How closely the cinema's first attempts at comedy were tied to this tradition is illustrated by a film of 1899, James Williamson's *Come Along Do!*, in which an old lady drags away her husband who is overly interested in a piece of nude female statuary in an art gallery. The film almost exactly duplicates a painting of 1862 by Stammell, inspired by a Venus exhibited in the International Exhibition of that year, and which had subsequently been popular-

*Come Along Do!* 1898

ized by a comic song, china fairing groups, stereoscope slides, magic lantern slides and, contemporary with the film, picture postcards. Thus a mildly suggestive pictorial joke of mid-Victorian times came to provide a theme for film comedy. Such a film as R. W. Paul's *Funny Faces*, whose title is entirely explanatory, derived from a tradition as old as painting. Lumiere's *Watering the Gardener*—made in 1896 and arguably the first film comedy— shows the maximum extent of narrative or gag in the primitive era. A naughty boy treads on the hose; the gardener peers down it and is soaked when the boy removes his foot. In G. A. Smith's *The Miller and the Sweep* the heroes fight, with the result that the miller becomes black and the sweep white.

9

As films became longer and public enthusiasm failed to decline as the pioneers had predicted, the dramatic possibilities of the medium were recognized. The action of comedies was elaborated; but for several years more their humour derived essentially from the action. What was funny was the happening, rather than the relationship to that happening of the people concerned. Naturally if someone pulled a chair from under someone else it seemed funnier if the culprit was a cheeky boy and his victim a fat lady or irascible old gentleman; and if the lady or gentleman waved his or her arms or otherwise expressed extravagant anger. Yet despite various hints—the music-hall comedians who occasionally re-corded fragments of their acts before the camera; the strong characterizations in Méliès' comic films—it was not until the middle of the first decade of this century that the clown proper, the figure who produces laughter by his relationship to the world and events around him, made his entry into the cinema.

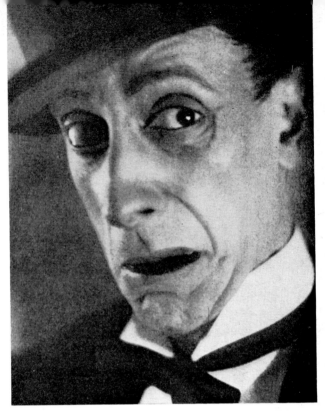

André Deed, *c.* 1912

### First flowering: France's comic empire

It was France—which dominated the world's cinema industry in the decade before the First World War—which gave clear definition to a genre of screen comedy in which the personality of the comic actor was central to the humour. The first true movie clown was André Deed (born, André Chapuis, in 1884), who brought to the cinema a training as music hall singer and acrobat, and something, too, of a whole ancient tradition of clowning that went back to the Italian Pierrot and the Augustes of the circus. Deed had occasionally played in films for Georges Méliès; but his film career properly dates from 1906, when Charles Pathé saw him on stage at the Châtelet Theatre and at once engaged him for a chase film, *La course à la perruque*. Deed went on to make a whole series of comedies; and within a matter of months his character of 'Boireau' was known throughout Europe. In 1908 —perhaps nervous at the fast-growing popularity of his rival star at Pathé, Max Linder—Deed accepted an offer to work for the Itala Film Company in Turin. There, as Cretinetti, he achieved the peak of his fame—an international celebrity which is not altogether easy for us to appreciate today, faced with the few scratched, faded, primitive fragments of five- and six-minute films which survive as evidence of Deed's work.

André Deed in an unidentified film, *c.* 1907

An odd feature of silent screen comedy was that each country gave its own local nickname to popular comedians. Thus in his Pathé days, while Deed was 'Boireau' at home, the Italians called him 'Beoncelli', the Spanish 'Sánchez' and so on. When he came to make films in Italy he became 'Cretinetti' there, whereupon the French renamed him 'Gribouille', the Spanish 'Toribio', the Russians 'Glupishkin' and the English 'Foolshead'. Deed, perhaps because of the change of identity in the move from France to Italy, never created a firmly defined personality as Linder and the later American comics were to do. His character tended to alter

André Deed in an unidentified film, c. 1909

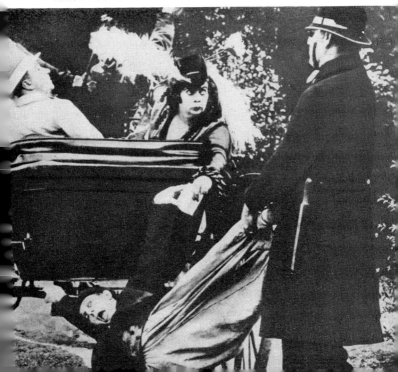

according to the immediate needs of the story. His magnificently insuperable idiocy alone was constant, often surrealist in its mindlessness and apocalyptic in its destruction. He is likely to pick-axe a hole in the wall in preference to using the door. His mere presence in a cinema ends in chaos. He brings home a Christmas tree with the candles ready lit, and burns down his own house. His rare inspirations of ingenuity were even more disconcerting. In *I Tacchi di Cretinetti*, finding it difficult to walk on the high heels he has adopted to increase his height, he walks on his hands instead.

At the Méliès studios Deed had learnt a lot about the craft of film-making, and particularly about comic magic. He was the first director-comedian to use all the humorous possibilities of accelerated action, magical appearances and disappearances and other comic trickery. A talented director, Deed continued to make films even after he ceased to be a star in his own right. But his career did not survive the advent of sound. One of the highest paid artists of the pre-war era, Deed ended his days as a nightwatchman at the Pathé Studios where he had once reigned.

André Deed, *Cretinetti al cinema*, 1911

Pathé had other comedians to succeed Deed after his defection to Italy. Charles Prince (1872–1933), with his great, clownish face and upturned nose, caricatured the comfortable bourgeoisie of pre-war France. Unhappily his films rarely equalled his richly comic looks. Neither Prince nor his director Monca had the creative gift of Deed or Linder; and the strain of producing a film every week was often betrayed by repetition and feeble comedy. Still, the age had an insatiable appetite for fun; and Prince—as 'Whiffles' in England, 'Prenz' in Russia, 'Moritz' in Germany, 'Selustiano' in Spain, 'Timofeo Tartufini' in Italy and 'Rigadin' at home in France—was no less successful than Deed. Other Pathé comedians were recruited from the music hall: Louis-Jacques Boucot, a favourite caff'concert singer with a melancholy face, epileptic movements and a disconcerting manner of suddenly obtruding his tongue, was known on the screen as 'Boucot', 'Peinard' and 'Gavroche' and survived to make feature-length comedies in the 'twenties; Dranem (1869–1935), one of the great stars of Parisian variety, made a series of films around 1908.

*Opposite*
Charles Prince, *Les Cendres*, 1911


Charles Prince, *Rigadin Manchot*, 1912

Roméo Bosetti had also played in vaudeville (his debut was at 10, as 'roi des casseurs d'assiettes') before joining Pathé in 1908. A resourceful director as well as a good comic, he moved to the rival firm of Gaumont for a few months; but in 1910 was put in charge of Pathé's new Comica Studios at Nice. Here his principal stars were Sablon, *alias* 'Babylas', and the tiny, grimacing German clown Little Moritz (the name was adapted from Prince's German nickname) whose films generally set him in pursuit of the statuesque Sarah Duhamel ('Rosalie'), who bravely endured the indignities devised by Bosetti's scenarios. Other Pathé stars were

Roméo Bosetti, *L'Invention du Tailleur*, 1910

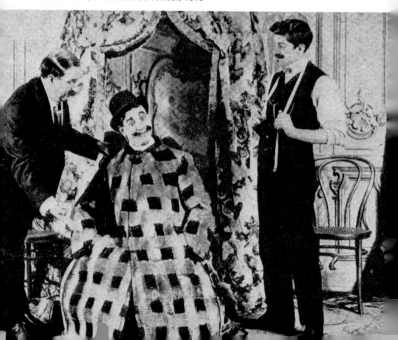

Cazalis (*alias* 'Jobard', *alias* 'Caze') and Leon Durac, who created the character of Nick Winter, a comic detective based disrespectfully on the popular Nick Carter, and inclined to find himself involved in such picturesque crimes as the larceny of the Mona Lisa.

At the Gaumont Studios, where the guiding artistic force was the great pioneer director of thrillers, Louis Feuillade (1873–1925), the tendency was to an altogether more extravagant kind of comedy. Gaumont comedies were prodigal with trick camerawork, with such fantasies as a runaway perambulator which crosses Paris,

Little Moritz, *Little Moritz se fait les muscles*, 1911

France and the ocean to land on a desert island; and with such pleasing incongruities as camels and horses in fashionable *salons*. The crazy images of the films of Onésime (Ernest Bourbon; though after 1916 the role passed to Marcel Levesque) and Calmo (Mige) clearly prefigure the surrealists; and René Clair's *Paris Qui Dort* unquestionably owes something to the fantasy of *Onésime Horloger*, in which time is telescoped, and all the activities of daily life are accelerated four-fold as a result of the hero's tampering with an electric clock in order to hasten the twenty years that he must wait for a legacy. As Léonce, Léonce Perret, a significant director of the French silent cinema, achieved great popularity in a series of comedies made between 1910 and 1912.

Under Feuillade's guidance Gaumont enjoyed great commercial success with a series of films starring two successive juvenile comedians, Bébé Abeilard and Bout-de-Zan, a horrid child who was maliciously (and perhaps unjustly) reputed to be a dwarf of advanced years; and who added to the merriment of those last days of the old pre-war world by the pranks he played on guileless elders.

Jean Durand, *Onésime aime les bêtes*, 1912

Jean Durand, *Onésime se bat en duel*, 1913

## Max Linder

Unique among the clowns of this first golden age, however, was the incomparable Max Linder who, more than any other artist, was to shape the whole future of film comedy. He was born Gabriel Levielle, in 1882, to a well-to-do family of Saint Loubès, near Bordeaux. Stage-struck, he studied at the Bordeaux Conservatoire, where he won prizes for tragedy as well as comedy. He acted for three years with the Théâtre des Arts in Bordeaux before going to Paris. Rejected by the Conservatoire, he joined the company of the Ambigu. In 1905 he began to augment his salary by working days at the Pathé Studios, for a flat 20 francs a day plus remuneration when his clothes were damaged, which—the comedies of those times being what they were—was often. The shame (for a legitimate stage actor) of playing in movies was mitigated by assuming the name Max Linder for his screen work.

For two years he was playing in as many as ten films a week, often only as an extra. His real chance came when Deed left Pathé for Italy, and Pathé decided to star Max in his own series. The earliest of these were tentative; it took a little time for the eventual character of Max to crystallize in its perfect form—the elegant young boulevardier, svelte, handsome, with sleek hair, neatly trimmed moustache, elegant cutaway, a beautiful cravat, the fanciest of fancy waistcoats and the shiniest of silk hats. Linder's Max was ingenious and intelligent: though his eye for the ladies was always getting him into some sort of trouble, he generally scraped his way out of it pretty successfully. His comic style was

Max Linder with Charles Chaplin in Hollywood, c. 1917

altogether novel. His predecessors were all in the narrowest sense clowns—grotesque in face and figure, and dressed in clothes that emphasized their absurdity. Max from the start perceived the comedy inherent in the contrast between his personal elegance and the ludicrous situations that befell him. Abandoning the frenetic and exaggerated activity of his contemporaries, Max's calm, controlled performance imposed upon his best films a distinctive, oddly syncopated rhythm.

Linder, more than any of the others, perceived the essential nature of the cinema, the essential demands of screen comedy. Though he came from the stage, his comedy style belonged uniquely to the screen with its possibilities for detail of gesture and expression and for technical tricks, though Linder used these sparingly and always to precise effect. His comic invention was prodigious. Between his debut and 1914 Linder made over four hundred films for Pathé. Some were very short; many were crude or repetitious. Yet overall his invention rarely flagged; and every comedian to this day has drawn, consciously or not, upon the vast repertory of gags which Linder built up in these years. Like all the great comedians, Max could extemporize endless variations upon a single activity like taking a bath, climbing a mountain, putting on a pair of tight shoes. Astonishingly, his films—unequal, but never careless in the matter of performance—were shot without retakes, after a single rehearsal of each scene.

Max's spectacular international success led to a series of European tours. But despite his popularity and astronomical earnings,

his life was shadowed. His already delicate health was impaired by war service, and his nervous system began to suffer. Engaged by the American Essanay company to replace Chaplin, whom they had lost to Mutual, his failure in America (probably largely due to Essanay's denigration of their former star; though Chaplin and Linder were personally friends, and Chaplin later acknowledged his own debt to Linder's work) was a further blow to his morale. Returning to France he played in only one film—Raymond Bernard's *Le Petit Café*—in the course of two years; but then, apparently with Chaplin's encouragement, he returned to the States, set up his own company and made three features which remain his masterpieces: *Seven Year's Bad Luck*, *Be My Wife* and

Max Linder, *Max Pedicure*, 1914

*The Three Must-Get-Theres*. The first of them is largely taken up with a single virtuoso gag involving a mirror which has lost its glass; the third, a parody of Fairbanks' *The Three Musketeers*, skilfully exploits the tricky *genre* of comic anachronism.

Yet even these marvellous films were only coolly received in America, and poor Max, by now prey to the comedian's traditional melancholia, returned to France. He made a film with Abel Gance, *Au Secours!*, and another in Vienna with Edouard-Emile Violet, *Le Roi du Cirque*. His brilliance was undiminished, but his mind wandered in a lonely darkness. He spoke of another picture; but early in the morning of 31 October 1925 Linder and his young wife, apparently in a suicide pact, took their own lives.

Max Linder, *The Three Must-Get-Theres*, 1922

# The French influence

The power of the Pathé empire in Europe meant that French comedy styles were dominant in the pre-war years. Rigadin, Onésime, Léonce, Boireau and their adventures were imitated and duplicated everywhere. In Italy, Deed's most serious rival was the endearingly quaint Ferdinando Guillaume (born 1887) who became in turn 'Tontolini', 'Cocciatelli' and 'Polidor' as he moved from one rival company to another in pursuit of higher rewards. As 'Robinet', Marcel Fabre had equal success before going to America to star in a series of Vim Comedies. After losing his arm in an accident, he was obliged to become a gag-man at Universal. He was followed to America by Emilio Vardannes, whose screen name of 'Toto' was later to be adopted by a more memorable Italian comic actor. In Germany the future director Ernst Lubitsch starred as 'Meyer' in a series of crude Jewish comedies.

*Opposite*
Ferdinando Guillaume, unidentified comedy, *c.* 1912

Ferdinando Guillaume, *Polidor Administers Injections*, 1912

Russia, where a strong Francophile culture still prevailed, easily adopted the French comic pattern; and the Russian usage which defined the grotesque caricature heroes of the primitive comic films as 'masks', suggests a significant parallel with the *maschi* of the old Italian *commedia*. One of the most successful pre-revolutionary comedians was the Pole, Antonin Fertner, whose creature Antosha—a foolish, improvident gallant—was inclined to fall into precisely the same embarrassments and predicaments as Deed or Prince. Several circus clowns achieved considerable

Antonin Fertner, *Antosha Wrecks a Pair of Corsets*, 1915

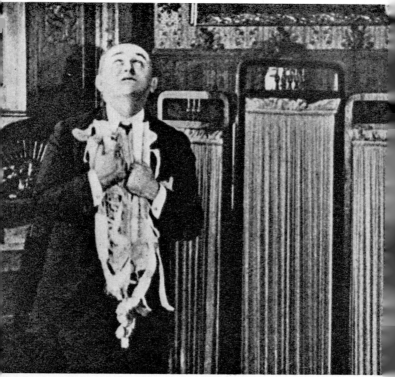

popularity in films, and their international origins indicate the overall lack of a real national comedy tradition in Russia. The clown Giacomino (1884–1956), for instance, was a Milanese; while Reynolds was clearly Anglo-Saxon. Only two artists seem to have embodied identifiably Slavic characters: V. Avdeyev's fat bourgeois, Djadja Pud, who was in constant comic counterpoint to a world that moved faster than his great bulk could follow; and N. P. Nirov's Mitjukha, a peasant youth, forever baffled before the mysteries of the big city.

Antonin Fertner, *Antosha and the Black Hand*, 1916

V. Avdeyev, *Djadja Pud—Terror of Wetnurses*, 1913

A little later than these, the work of Arkady Boitler betrayed the combined influence of Linder—whose personal appearances in Russia* had aroused immense public enthusiasm—and Chaplin.

* Linder presented a stage act which was largely improvised. This placed considerable demands on the pianists engaged to accompany him. In St Petersburg his accompanist was an unknown but brilliant young performer named Dimitri Tiomkin, later to become one of Hollywood's best-known film composers.

Arkady Boitler, *Arkasha Marries*, 1917

The elegance, sophistication and urban savoir-faire of Boitler's 'Arkasha' and the restraint and perceptive psychology of his playing were very much closer to Linder than to any of the Russian comedian's compatriot predecessors.

Will Evans, *c.* 1915

In Britain, meanwhile, film comedy had scarcely evolved from the primitive animated picture postcards of the early years of the century: the few English clowns who appeared in film series, though they enjoyed enormous popularity at home, possessed none of Linder's sophistication or appreciation of the special needs and properties of the cinema. The popular music-hall comedian Will Evans attempted to transfer some of his stage sketches to the screen, even though most of his appeal lay in the absurd dialogue and asides of his stage performances. His nephew Fred Evans, with an absurdly clownish face and a rather unsubtle line in knockabout, enjoyed a more sustained success in the immediate pre-war and wartime period with his 'Pimple' series, which tended to topicality in the choice of themes. Few of the Pimple films really invite revival, though the titles are often engaging: *Miss Pimple—Suffragette, Pimple Up the Pole, Pimple Enlists, Pimple's Wonderful Gramophone, Pimple the Bad Girl of the Family.* The success of the Pimple series attracted competitors: the Yorkshire Film Company had its 'Winky' series; while Clarendon Films made a series starring a comic called 'Jack Spratt'.

America too lagged behind continental Europe. Surprisingly, in view of the strong vaudeville tradition on which it had to draw and the immense popularity of funny films, the output of comedies before 1910 was small and their quality rather worse than puerile. Around 1910 the American Mutoscope company experimented with clown heroes in the European style; but neither 'Jonesy' nor

Fred Evans, *Pimple's Wonderful Gramophone*, 1913

'Bumptious', a plump and pompous little man, achieved either the solid characterization or the lasting popularity of Max or even Cretinetti. But in the same year the Vitagraph Company launched the first American comic star, John Bunny. Bunny (1863–1915) had been a successful actor and manager. With remarkable foresight he perceived the potential of moving pictures, and in 1910 offered his services to the Vitagraph Company. At first unenthusiastic, by the end of a year or so Vitagraph were grateful to pay Bunny a thousand dollars a week. Bunny was rotund and genial, with a large and irresistibly comical face. His films tended to centre on social mix-ups and domestic embarrassments in which he was caught between his own incorrigible amorousness and the domination of his plain and ferocious wife, played by Flora Finch. Bunny died in 1915, and the subsequent failure to make stars out of his various collaborators indicates that he was a comedian of unique talent and not just a happy grotesque. His brother, George Bunny, who bore a strong resemblance to the comedian, failed utterly when he made a few films for Goldwyn in 1918. Hughie Mack, a gross young man who had appeared with Bunny from 1913, made a few slapstick films on his own account, with small success; and Flora Finch's career never recovered

*Opposite*
John Bunny in costume, *c.* 1912

John Bunny at the Vitagraph Studios, *c.* 1914

V. Zimovoi, *Poxon up the Volga*, 1915

after her partner's death, even though she operated her own producing company for a while. Bunny's popularity launched American film comedy into the European market. So great was his popularity in Russia, for instance, where he was known as 'Poxon', that after his death a Russian Poxon, V. Zimovoi, was created in a vain attempt to replace him.

The American film industry—particularly in those days of cut-throat company wars—has never needed more than a single success to launch an avalanche of imitation. From 1910 comedy stars began to proliferate—the best of them drawn, inevitably, from the rich reserves of vaudeville. Initially, however, Vitagraph enjoyed more success with the pictures of Mr and Mrs Sydney Drew—like the Carter De Havens a few years later, less comedians than players of light comedy—than with broader clowns like Billy Quirk and the English, ex-Karno comedian, Jimmie Aubrey.

The Essanay Company developed an authentically native style in the Snakeville Comedies that, from 1910 and throughout the

Wallace Beery and Gloria Swanson, *c.* 1916

war, created characters from a comic-strip wild west, including most notably Augustus Carney's Alkali Ike and William Todd's Mustang Pete. Essanay also promoted a supporting player, Wallace Beery, to star in the very popular 'Sweedie' series; though the company's triumph was their capture of Charlie Chaplin from Sennett's Keystone Studios in 1915. Every American company tried comedy. Selig imitated Snakeville with a 'Bloom Centre' series. Kalem teamed Lloyd V. Hamilton and Bud Duncan as a knockabout hobo team, generally directed by the erratic but gifted Marshall Neilan. Hobo acts had long been popular in vaudeville, and other teams, with names like Poke and Jabbs or Plump and Runt, were thrust into film series. In 1911 the Nestor Film Company translated Bud Fisher's strip cartoon characters Mutt and Jeff to the screen, with actors playing the two heroes: in later years Mutt and Jeff were to have a more sustained success in animated cartoons. Comedies and comedians proved the most effective ammunition in the industrial wars of the pre-1914 American cinema; and artists of all kinds and qualities appeared and vanished and changed sides in the ever-altering landscape of film companies that mushroomed and vanished, amalgamated, split and re-formed before the clearer lines of the Hollywood industry were defined in the middle 'twenties.

## An art of lunacy: Sennett and Keystone

The most conspicuously successful comedy company was, however, Keystone, formed by Mack Sennett with the backing of
Adam Kessel and Charles Bauman, two bookmakers. Sennett was
Canadian, of Irish descent. After trying his luck as a singer, he
joined Biograph as an actor in 1908 and took pains to study the
methods of Biograph's star director, D. W. Griffith. By 1910 he was
himself directing, and in 1912 launched into autocratic and
idiosyncratic production at Keystone. Whether Sennett hit by
happy chance upon a formula, or actually had a unique genius as
a creative producer, Keystone developed under his rule its own
inimitable and immortal genre of surreal visual comedy. It enriched the folk-lore of America and the world, with the Keystone
Kops and all the other curious and colourful characters who
peopled the Sennett universe; and (quite incidentally to Sennett's
aims, which were simply to turn comedy into a commercial com-
modity) made an invaluable contribution to cinema art by giving
a new rhythm and fluidity to film editing, and a new freedom to the
camera which had to develop the agility to catch the clowns where
they fell, or to follow them into the depths of the endless land-
scapes whence their breakneck chases were liable to lead.

Sennett recruited his artists from burlesque, circus, vaudeville,
building sites, mental hospitals. At first he directed all the films
himself; but as the Keystone output grew to keep several units
occupied at any one time, he employed other directors (often
recruited on the spur of the moment from among writers or actors
who happened to be handy and momentarily unemployed),
building a tower at the centre of his studios so that he could super-
vise everything that was happening at any particular moment.
Visitors—and some employees too—were convinced that the
Sennett lot was a madhouse. A troupe of show-off comedians
were constantly occupied in trying to outshine one another in
invention, dexterity and risk. For a laugh they would merrily throw
themselves off buildings, leap under trains, get hit with mallets or
drive motor-cars into house-sides. (The only recorded fatality, it is
said, had the merit of not being noticeable in the finished picture.)
The films were largely improvised; and a single prop (car, telephone, boat) or setting (grocery store, garage, kitchen or bedroom)

The Keystone Kops, *In the Clutches of the Gang*, 1914 : extreme left, Ford Sterling ; right, Fatty Arbuckle

was sufficient to set off seemingly endless enchaînements of comedy. Sometimes there were story conferences (though they did not necessarily affect what ultimately went into the picture) and James Agee has left a famous account of the 'Wild Man' Sennett is said to have employed for these : 'an all but brainless, speechless man, scarcely able to communicate his ideas : but he had a totally uninhibited imagination. He might say nothing for an hour ; then he'd mutter "You take this cloud . . ." Often he could get no further, but thanks to some kind of thought-transference, saner men would take this cloud and make something of it' (*Life*, 3 September 1949).

The outcome of this seeming chaos was a genre of film comedy that drew on comic strips, on the early French cinema clowns, the *commedia dell'arte*, vaudeville, pantomime ; and yet was different from all of these, and unique. The Keystone comedies remain a monument of twentieth-century popular art, transmuting the evident surfaces of the life and times of the 'teens and 'twenties of the century into a manner of comedy that is basic and universal. Like all the best comedy, the Sennett shorts were uncompromisingly anarchic. In an era of determinedly materialistic values, the Sennett films celebrated orgiastic destruction of goods and possessions, of cars and houses and crockery. Authority and dignity counted for nothing. Never was authority more utterly reduced than by the Keystone Kops, that supremely incompetent force who were endlessly tumbling down steps, falling out of windows, flying under the impulse of centrifugal force off patrol wagons that skidded round corners at 100 miles an hour, ran brakeless and beyond control down 45 degree hillsides and ultimately rocketed off cliff-edges.

The Keystone Kops, *c*. 1916

The inhabitants of this world were larger and wilder and more colourful than life. They might be fat or thin, giants or dwarfs, with oversize pants and undersize hats, tangled spectacles and overgrown moustaches; but in any case they were ridiculous, monstrous, adorable caricatures of reality. Sennett's earliest stars were Mabel Normand, Ford Sterling and Fred Mace. Normand was in a class by herself, among the Keystone troupe, in that she never had recourse to grotesque effects or make-up to be funny. She was beautiful, vital, possessed of an incomparable gift for mimicry and an ability to appear completely natural before the camera. Sennett, whose personal affection for her outlasted her life to his own death, starred her in several features, the best of which is *Mickey*, in which she brings Keystone humour to a Pickford orphan role. Normand's personal life was colourful but troubled; and she died from tuberculosis at the age of 36, in 1930.

Fred Mace was obese and slow-thinking, a useful foil for Ford Sterling, the habitual Superintendant of the Keystone Kops, with his wry, cross face ornamented with a small goatee; and a frenzied, leaping, grimacing line in comedy. In the years that followed* Sennett turned over a notable army of comics. (Fearful of starting a wage escalation he would never pay enough to keep his most successful stars for long: he lost his greatest discovery, Chaplin, after only a year and thirty-five one- or two-reel pictures.) Outside the great stars—Chaplin, Langdon, Lloyd—who first appeared with Sennett, two of his most celebrated *alumni* were Roscoe (Fatty) Arbuckle and Ben Turpin. Arbuckle's career was abruptly ended by a scandal in 1921, when a girl died following a party which he had thrown in a San Francisco Hotel. Arbuckle was

* In 1915 Keystone became a producing entity within the Triangle Company. In 1917 Sennett left Triangle to release through Paramount and subsequently through Associated Producers, First National and, from 1923, through Pathé.

Mabel Normand, William Jefferson and Al St John, *He Did and He Didn't*, 1916

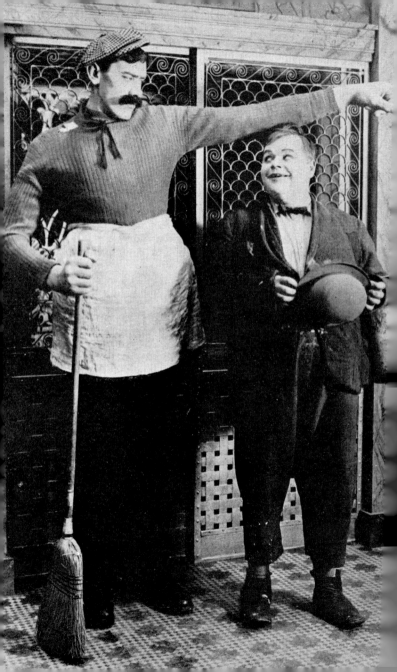

subsequently acquitted of manslaughter, but public opinion forced him to retire from the screen, and the shadow of death and orgy seems still to lie upon the innocent fun of such of his work as has survived. But his contemporaries loved him. He was huge and baby-faced and bouncy, forever countering misfortune with ingenuity in the pursuit of his heroine—whom he invariably won in the end. The joy of Arbuckle was his agility—always funny in a fat person—and his phenomenal dexterity. He could roll a cigarette with one hand, accurately aim knives backwards over his shoulder, and shy custard pies with lethal precision in two directions at once. He enjoyed female disguises, and was irresistibly funny galloping up the dust roads of 1917 Los Angeles dressed as a balloon-sized Mary Pickford. Practically from the first, Arbuckle directed his own films, and Buster Keaton admitted that his own skill as a director had been learnt from him. Arbuckle's foil at Keystone and later, after he had formed his own company, was Al St John, a comic of more energy than subtlety whose career as a supporting player extended into the 1950s.

*Opposite*
Michael Grealis and Fatty Arbuckle, *His Wife's Mistake*, 1916

Fatty Arbuckle, *Those Country Kids*, 1914

Ben Turpin was a supremely ridiculous figure: undersized, stringy, his whole being seeming to orbit about a hugely expressive Adam's-apple which, in moments of crisis or passion, Ben seemed to protrude as other men throw out their chests. His fortune lay in his remarkable eyes: hopelessly and definitively crossed, their sightlines clashed at a point barely an inch before his nose. Born in 1868 or 1872, he was one of the earliest American film comedians, having joined Essanay first in 1907. Thereafter he worked in circuses but returned to play in Snakeville comedies and sub-

Fatty Arbuckle, *Fatty's Hoodoo Day*, 1914

sequently in some of the Essanay Chaplin shorts. His fame came when Sennett exploited his acrobatic ability, his incomparably ludicrous physique and his gift for parody, in films with titles like *East Lynne with Variations, Uncle Tom Without the Cabin, The Shriek of Araby* (with Turpin as Valentino) and *Three Foolish Weeks* (Turpin as Von Stroheim). A thorough-going eccentric, Turpin is said to have acted as janitor in his own apartment house and to have always travelled by bus, announcing his entry with a shrill squeak of 'I'm Ben Turpin—earn three thousand dollars a week!'

Ben Turpin, *The Prodigal Bridegroom*, 1926

Charlie Chase was long and gangly, with a look of hurt bewilderment, a foolish little moustache and a vague air of being assembled of slightly ill-fitting parts. Though he started at Keystone, and later made silent films for Roach, his principal success came in the early years of talking pictures. As Charles Parrott he was a gifted director of comedy. Little Billy Bevan, with his hurt dignity and outsize moustache, remained with Sennett for many years. Hideous moustaches were also the making of Chester Conklin and Mack Swain, who frequently appeared together as rivals in love for some hapless Keystone heroine—Marie Prevost, perhaps, or

*Opposite*
Charlie Chase with tango partner

May Wells, Mack Swain, Harry Gribbon, Julia Faye, *His Auto-Ruination*, 1916

Phyllis Haver. Intended for the Church, Conklin left home to go on the stage ; and originally adopted the moustache as an appropriate prop for a 'German' comic act. Later he toured with circuses until he signed with Sennett in 1913. Always eager for legitimate roles, Conklin played the father of Zasu Pitts in Von Stroheim's *Greed*. In later years, in *Modern Times* and *The Great Dictator*, he resumed an association that dated back to Chaplin's first films of 1914. Conklin continued to appear in character roles until 1960.

The Sennett Studios were, indeed, an unmatchable school. Keystone stars and debutants at various times included Charles Murray, George (Slim) Summerville, Charlie Chaplin's brother

Chester Conklin and Charles Chaplin, *Modern Times*, 1936, directed by Charles Chaplin

Sydney, Hank Mann, Edgar Kennedy, Harry McCoy, Raymond Hitchcock, Harry Brooks, Don Barclay, Harry Booker, Francis Wilson and Billy Walsh. At least two Keystone Kops—Eddie Sutherland and Edward Cline—became distinguished comedy directors, as did two Keystone gag-men, Malcolm St Clair and Frank Capra. There were funny women at Sennett too, apart from the bewitching Mabel Normand. Louise Fazenda was hardly less attractive than Mabel, but managed successfully to obscure the fact with her absurd hairdos and extravagantly dowdy clothes. Polly Moran in later years became an excellent foil to Marie Dressler. The regular company also included Minta Durfee, Alice Davenport,

Louise Fazenda, *Tillie's Punctured Romance*, 1928

Phyllis Allen and Alice Howell, of the fuzzy hair and turned-out feet. Though Sennett's bathing beauties were chosen for their sex-appeal and publicity value, comedy seemed infectious and such former Sennett girls as Gloria Swanson, Phyllis Haver and Marie Prevost developed into talented comediennes.

Sennett's most serious rival was Hal Roach, who launched himself as a producer when he perceived the comedy potential of Harold Lloyd. In 1918 Roach made a series of films with the Italian comic Toto, and about the same time engaged Stan Laurel and the balding, scraggy, sour-faced James Finlayson—later the villain of countless Laurel and Hardy films—who had arrived in the States with the English touring company of *Bunty Pulls the Strings*. By 1923 Roach had become ambitious enough to engage the popular stage comedian Will Rogers. Although he made a great number of successful silent films, however, Rogers' folksy, rural American humour depended upon speech, and his most durable work was done in talking pictures.

Phyllis Haver in an unidentified Keystone comedy, *c.* 1917

The complete roster of slapstick comedians who came to the screen in the last decade of the silent cinema is too large even to number. Among them—apart from the Keystone troupe—were Clyde Cook, Bobby Vernon, Ralph Graves and Raymond McKee, Wally Van, William Wadsworth, Charley Bowers, Glenn Tryon, Billie Ritchie, Snub Pollard, Andy Clyde, Earle Fox, Dutch Walsh and Raymond Hatton. The funny ladies who disputed the theory that slapstick is not a game for women included Dot Farley, who claimed to be the ugliest woman in pictures (though apart from a remarkable fan of teeth she was not all that bad), Fay Tincher, Mae Busch—later the angriest of all the Laurel and Hardy angry wives—and the virago Kate Price, whose most memorable appearance is in *My Wife's Relations*, as the big Irish busy-body who catches Buster Keaton breaking a window and hauls him before a magistrate who cannot speak English so promptly marries them.

James Finlayson and Phyllis Haver in an unidentified comedy, *c.* 1917

One of the most elusive talents of silent comedy, Larry Semon seemed to reincarnate the Pierrot Lunaire of Debureau. His face was a white mask with sharp little points of eyes, and a quirky, upturned smile. He began his career as a newspaper cartoonist, but joined Vitagraph as a writer and director. A great gag-man, Semon's films touched a kind of surrealism that perhaps prevented the development of a consistent and identifiable character. Keaton shrewdly pointed out that you could never remember a Semon film after you had seen it because (unlike Keaton himself) Semon did not let the gags grow naturally out of the story or character, but strung them together in disconnected and illogical chains. The more successful Semon grew, the more he worried about his reputation and his popularity. The worry inevitably told, in turn, upon his work. Forced to produce independently, he became less and less successful in his later films, until by 1928 he was declared bankrupt. Later the same year he died—of worry, his friends said— aged only 39.

*Below and opposite*
Larry Semon, in his last film *Spuds*, 1928

Monty Banks (Monte Bianchi) emigrated from Italy to the States as a youth. A stylish comic in the elegant, dapper Linder–Raymond Griffith manner, he later became a notable director of comedy. Another immigrant, Lupino Lane was much more successful in his American films than when he worked in British studios. A deft acrobat and dexterous with visual comic business, Lane seems never to have balanced his physical comedy with a sufficiently marked comic personality. A vaguely troubled innocent, the face he presented was not unlike Langdon's but without any of Langdon's poetry or mystery. Lane's brother Wallace Lupino also appeared in a few two-reel comedies.

Lupino Lane, *Naughty Boy*, 1927

The success of film comedy attracted a good many transients from the theatre. In 1914 Marie Dressler appeared in *Tillie's Punctured Romance,* an adaptation of her stage success *Tillie's Nightmare*, at Keystone, where she co-starred with Chaplin and Normand. Weber and Fields, Eddie Foy and Joe Jackson were also won by Sennett. Victor Moore made feature comedies for Lasky; W. C. Fields, the great comedy juggler, appeared in one or two pictures for Casino Star Comedies, though both comedians were to achieve more substantial success in sound pictures.

The 'twenties also saw a revival of juvenile comedies. Sunny McKeen was already starring in the *Baby Snookums* series at the age of one and a half. The *Mickey McGuire* films introduced a boy comedian of that name who was later to achieve fame as Mickey Rooney. Hal Roach's *Our Gang* series starred a whole juvenile troupe, established its own folk-lore and inspired several perfectly forgettable imitations.

Attempts to establish a British tradition of silent slapstick comedy equivalent to the American were never sustained or successful—surprisingly in view of the strong comic traditions of the British music hall. As early as 1915 a group of music-hall artists had formed Homeland Films, but the various series of one- or two-reelers made with Charlie Austin ('Parker P. C.'), Billy Merson and Winifred Dalvanti are forgotten. In the same year Lupino Lane had formed Little Nipper Films. Bertie Wright, a musical comedy artist and the brother of Huntley Wright, achieved some popularity as 'Bertie' in a series of *Moonshine Comedies*; Betty Balfour was a charming and vivacious comedienne in George Pearson's *Squibs* series; the famous pantomime clown Whimsical Walker appeared in a series of shorts for Hepworth; George Robey attempted to translate his distinctive comedy style to the cinema. Essentially, however, Britain lacked a producer with Sennett's eye for broad comedy and his uninhibited approach to the art and business of film-making. In the 'twenties the nearest approach to a true film comedy was the films of Walter Forde— clearly deeply influenced by Harold Lloyd, but already revealing something of the talent that was to make Forde an excellent director of comedy films in the 'thirties.

Marie Dressler, Charles Chaplin and Mabel Normand, *Tillie's Punctured Romance*, 1915

# Apogee: Chaplin, Keaton, Lloyd, Langdon and others

The single decade that preceded the introduction of talking pictures saw the appearance of four figures of dazzling brilliance and unprecedented universal appeal. Like the Elizabethan theatre or the *commedia dell'arte* this flowering can only partly be attributed to the fate and chance of time that brought particular talents to a particular place at a specific period. There were quite sound historical reasons also. The silent cinema, as we have seen, reached the peak of its art and assurance in time to take advantage of the culmination of a rich tradition of popular comic theatre. This fortunately happened also at a period just before the demands of big business and industrial evolution subjected film-makers to pressures totally inimical to the sort of independence and autonomy that is essential to artistic creation in any medium. The great comedians were masters of their medium organizationally and economically, as well as technically. In later years Buster Keaton expressed regret at 'the lackadaisical working habits of many modern comedy stars . . . We stayed with the story all the way. In the old days all of us—Chaplin, Lloyd, Harry Langdon and myself—worked with our writers from the day they started on a story. We checked on the scenery, the cast, the locations. . . . We directed our own pictures, making up our gags as we went along, saw the rushes, supervised the cutting, went to the sneak previews.'

Chaplin's tramp is the single truly universal clown image. The little bowler, the too-small jacket and the too-large pants held up with string, the enormous boots on turned-out feet, the moustache and cane are everywhere, instantly recognized and internationally comprehensible. The child of struggling variety artists—the father a wastrel, the mother a sensitive woman of precarious mental health—as a very small child Chaplin knew the miseries of a Victorian London of mean streets and institutions which seem to belong to Dickens' day rather than to living memory. From these facts of his life Chaplin's films derive their Dickensian atmospheres, perceptions, sentiments and morality; and it was from his childhood experiences that Chaplin gained his vision of the world of the underprivileged—a vision that was romanticized, transmuted into comedy, but ultimately rooted in inescapable truth.

Charles Chaplin, *c.* 1915

Chaplin went on the stage as a child and his long apprenticeship on the halls sharpened his techniques to wonderful precision and versatility. He possessed instinctive grace and rhythmic sense, a rare invention, a genuinely poetic instinct, a gift for mimicry and, ultimately, the quality of a great actor. (A good clown really *could* play Hamlet.) When Sennett recruited him late in 1913, Chaplin was touring the States with Fred Karno's *Mumming Birds*, in which his co-stars included Stan Laurel. His first film for Sennett cast him as a broken-down dandy in monocle and silk hat; but already in his second picture he had adopted the costume and begun to sketch the persona which was to bring him world fame. The character was to be refined and elaborated of course; the hero of *City Lights* or *Modern Times* is altogether more complex than the little tramp of the first frantic Sennett slapsticks as he scutters on one leg around corners, clutching his hat to his head while being chased by Keystone Kops or angry, whiskered giants. But the general lines of the character—the range of emotion from callousness to high sentiment and of his actions from nobility to larceny; the supremely human resilience and fallibility of his nature—were fairly soon defined.

Just as Linder's restrained style had broken away from his predecessors, Chaplin's relaxed, economical, totally accurate comedy was in striking contrast to the mugging and leaping of Ford Sterling, whom he replaced as Sennett's top star; and indeed at first the Sennett troupe rather doubted whether the little Englishman was funny at all. His speed and invention and subtlety were astonishing. Every prop inspired a string of gags; every action was precise and funny; and the richest comedy lay in the character itself, his expressive and immediate reactions to all that happened to him. Chaplin's most characteristic comedy lay in allusion. Every object or activity suggested to his quick eye for association, something else. In *The Pawnshop* an alarm-clock which he is examining suggests in rapid succession a can of beans, a wrist watch, a patient under medical examination, a tin of fishing worms. In *The Gold Rush* the starving Charlie is reduced to stewing and eating an old boot: the nails are daintily sucked like chicken bones and the laces become spaghetti.

Phyllis Allen, Mabel Normand, Mack Swain and Charles Chaplin, *His Trysting Place*, 1914

There were serious illuminations in Chaplin's work too. *Shoulder Arms*, metamorphosing the horror of mud and vermin and trench feet into high comedy, nowadays tells us more poignantly what that first war was like than many more serious dramatic films. However naïve and over-simplified the humanist philosophizing of his later films may seem, *Modern Times* is even today as valid a reflection as any upon the survival of personality in automated societies; and *The Great Dictator's* assertion of the survival of humanity under totalitarian dictatorships is today no less meaningful than in 1941.

Charles and (on right) Sydney Chaplin, *Shoulder Arms*, 1918

Charles Chaplin and Jack Oakie, *The Great Dictator*, 1941

The last decade has seen a sharp decline in Chaplin's critical reputation. It is an unjust but perhaps inevitable reaction against the intense critical adulation of the 'thirties and 'forties. His simple philosophies are out of key with the times, while his political unpopularity in America has had inevitable repercussions even among people who would most strenuously resist, in its origins, the intolerance and witch-hunting to which he was subjected. Nor have his own attitudes—his devotion to his own legend and fascination with his own celebrity; his growing refusal to acknowledge his debt, however minimal, to other artists—helped to dispel a reaction which has turned to positive antagonism with the comparative failure of the films of his old age, *A King in New York* and *A Countess From Hong Kong*.

This devaluation of Chaplin has been bound up with a growing recognition of the overwhelming talent of Buster Keaton. As a director Keaton was unquestionably Chaplin's superior. Chaplin learned his filmcraft well in 1914–15, and has never seen any reason to sophisticate techniques and styles which have always provided a serviceable arena for his talents as performer. Keaton was, all else apart, a great *metteur-en-scène*, using the medium with a fluency which few directors have mastered.

Like Chaplin, Keaton came to the cinema from the music hall, but the circumstances of his life were unique in that he joined the family vaudeville act almost before he could walk, and never knew any other way of life. As part of the family act, which for most of his youth was in good work, he had never any of the economic or social distractions which dogged the young Chaplin. To make comedy and solve stage problems was a way of life for him, excluding practically everything else.

It is already clear in the earliest films Keaton made with Roscoe Arbuckle how complete an equipment he had developed in vaudeville. The Arbuckle films improved immeasurably in quality and restraint during the year or so that Keaton was with the company. His own unique gifts finally matured, however, when he achieved the independence of his own studios. In the years between 1920 and 1928 he made a body of some score of two-reel shorts and twelve feature films which represent a truly staggering achievement. His invention never flags; he hardly ever repeats himself except to improve upon a gag.

Keaton was, above all else, an accomplished actor. Unlike the other great comedians of his day he developed a wide range of different characters. In *The Boat* he is husband and father; in *College* and *Steamboat Bill Jr* he is a college boy son. In several of his films he plays millionaires; in others he is a fugitive bum. In *Go West* he becomes a cow-hand; in *The Saphead* he becomes a stockbroker. He gave each character its own, self-centred validity; and yet in the end they all fuse into one divine figure, and become Buster: a game, ridiculous little animal, generally with a flat hat clamped down on its head, stumping along on stiff short legs, with arms that are inclined to start into sudden motion like a windmill; and, at the centre of all the activity, a still, sad face that is absurdly solemn and uniquely beautiful.

Buston Keaton on set, *c.* 1920

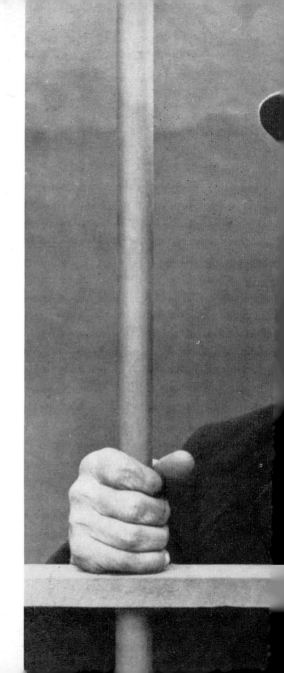

Buster Keaton
*The Goat,*
1921

'The Great Stone Face' is, though, a groundless myth. Buster's was the most expressive face in films. Asked why he never smiled, he once answered, 'I had other ways of showing I was happy'. A slow blink can express a climax of joy; and when at the end of *The Three Ages* he gets the girl and celebrates by throwing his hat, rather sedately, into the air, his ecstacy is explosive. He can be poignant, too; but never maudlin. In the end Buster always triumphs; for though he is small and alone and vulnerable, he is also self-reliant, indomitable, endlessly resourceful. Fate may help, but it is essentially his own ingenuity that wins in the end over the seemingly insuperable. The characteristic Keaton plot situation confronts the unaided, strictly human hero with some superhuman problem. In *The Navigator*, chance finds him adrift alone with his girl on an ocean liner whose whole equipment is geared to the use of a thousand people rather than two. In *The General*, he is a Southerner in the Civil War, single-handed against all the armies of the North. In *Seven Chances*, he has half a day to find a bride.

*Opposite*
Buster Keaton, *Battling Butler*, 1926

Buster Keaton, *Our Hospitality*, 1923

From childhood Keaton was fascinated by mechanical problems and mechanical devices. He loved machinery, and inventing things. Hence his rapid assimilation of the techniques of movie-making and his astonishing subsequent mastery of cinema method. This mastery lay not only in his use of camera and process tricks (some of which have never been surpassed or even explained). More important, his solution of every problem of *mise-en-scène* is unerringly correct. He possessed an impeccable sense of comic structure. Gags were never simply tacked on to the fabric of his films, but were germane to the narrative and a dynamic element in it. Within the gags themselves there is the same impeccable sense of structure, the same fascination with mechanical engineering. The gags of the mature films are built up as enchaînements of geometric and dynamic design, elegant, polished, rhythmical. From his entry into feature production in 1923 Keaton can be reckoned the equal of any film director then working in Hollywood.

While the comic characters of both Chaplin and Keaton seemed to emerge almost fully formed at the very start of their screen careers, the comedy personality of Harold Lloyd was a gradual evolution. Unlike the other three giants of the golden age of American comedy, Lloyd did not come from vaudeville. He had first tried his luck in legitimate drama, but been advised by Charlie Ruggles that he would make 'a better comedian than an Irving'; and had met Hal Roach when they were both earning five dollars a day as extras at Universal Studios. Later Roach went into production with a small legacy, and engaged Lloyd as a comic at three dollars a day. They settled on a tramp character, 'Willie Work', for Lloyd; but Lloyd left Roach for Sennett after a disagreement. However, when the Keystone troupe failed to see the funny side of him, he returned, to work out a character called 'Lonesome Luke'—a vaguely Chaplinesque hayseed hobo, with ludicrously ill-fitting clothes and a tiny moustache. The films, released by Pathé, gradually built up their popularity, and for two years (and something like two or three hundred shorts) Lloyd concentrated on the Lonesome Luke character until, in a one-reeler of 1917, *Over the Fence*, he adopted the horn-rimmed glasses and the brash and breezy air that were to bring him lasting fame.

Harold Lloyd on set, *c.* 1923

Gradually the characteristic form of his films and the characteristic personality of his hero became more clearly defined. Lloyd
was always the all-American boy, a true disciple of Horatio Alger,
a born go-getter. Whatever the ultimate motive (usually the need
to win a girl) his films are all built upon the hero's drive for social
or economic betterment. One suspects a sincere moral belief
behind the comedies—partly from Lloyd's real-life embodiment of
the success story (unlike most of his contemporaries he invested
his money well and is today very rich) ; partly from the way he
speaks of his films. Of his first feature, *A Tailor Made Man,* he
wrote, 'So you see the central idea was a real one : that hard knocks
will bring out a man's mettle if he has any.' In *Grandma's Boy* a
softy is transformed into a hero through the inspiration of a fic-
tional legend of his grandfather's bravery in the Civil War ; but 'the
boy discovers, of course, that he triumphed only because he be-
lieved in himself.'

The prissy go-getter would be unattractive, even unbearable,
but for Lloyd's odd but quite exceptional charm, and the highly
polished comedy skills he had developed in his early apprenticeship with Roach shorts. He could achieve his effects with great
economy. He has only to stand and stare in blank dismay at some
catastrophe of which he is the innocent cause, or to let his large,
confident, full-toothed smile wither into an agonized crumpled
line, to be extremely funny.

Harold Lloyd, *Why Worry ?,* 1926

His best-remembered gags were, of course, rather more strenuously achieved. Lloyd is always associated with the comedy of thrills and those awe-inspiring climactic feats of acrobatics in which the suspense (literally) was maintained for as much as a third of the film. The greatest of these is, of course, in *Safety Last,* in which Lloyd's need to impress his girl has in some unfortunate way resulted in his standing in for a human fly. He performs terrifying feats on the side of a skyscraper, twenty storeys above the roaring streets of the city. Trying to regain the safety of the roof, he is severely and successively hampered by a net, a mouse, a painters' lift, swinging windows, a clock which progressively disintegrates as he clutches first at its hands and then its face, and curious bystanders who offer supremely unhelpful criticisms. Lloyd formalized a method of comedy which has been the stock-in-trade of

The Plaza Cinema, Piccadilly Circus, at the time of the first British release of *Feet First*, 1930

Harry Langdon and Vernon Bent, *Picking Peaches*, 1924

screen comedians ever since; but neither he nor anyone else ever again achieved the rhythmic brilliance, the amazing, controlled crescendo of *Safety Last*.

Harry Langdon can hardly be reckoned the full equal of Chaplin, Keaton and Lloyd: his output was smaller and more uneven; his best work was generally due to the collaboration of good directors. But he was, as a clown, a great original. Born in 1884, the son of Salvation Army officers, he had been a cartoonist, prop boy, barber, medicine show performer and toured in vaudeville for twenty years with an act called 'Jimmy's New Car' before he joined Mack Sennett in 1923. He played in a number of two-reelers, but did not develop his unique screen character until Frank Capra, then a gag-writer with Sennett, devised *Tramp, Tramp, Tramp* for him. Subsequently Capra directed his best two films, *The Strong Man* and *Long Pants*.

Langdon is quieter, cuter, weirder than any of his contemporaries. He is on the one hand a kind of pierrot, with a white moon face and features starkly drawn; on the other, as James Agee pointed out, an elderly baby. His clothes are baby-like: tiny boots on out-turned feet; a squashed round hat that sits where it has been perched atop his head, turned up all round and with a half-formed kiss-curl creeping under it; flared and baggy trousers; an out-grown jacket with six buttons, the top one done up a bit awry at the top of his chest so that it all sticks out below, over his plump little body. His arms are stiff like a baby's, and won't lie flat by his sides; and his hands are podgy and clumsy until you see them close and realize with a slight turn that they are the hands of a middle-aged man.

Like a baby, he seems always to be being picked up or put down, dressed (by his boss in *The Strong Man*) or undressed (by a floozie in the same film). If he does attend to himself (rubbing his chest, for instance, with Limburger cheese under the impression that it is a cold cure), it is with the absorbed, erroneous care of a little child. And his mischief is a child's: *The Strong Man* opens with Harry as a First World War soldier, gleefully bombarding the enemy with ration biscuits hurled from a catapult.

The baby character gives an eerie edge to blacker moments of comedy, and makes his sexual encounters peculiar in the extreme. Langdon's whole comic quality is the apposition of baby innocence and the grown-up world in which life has landed him. His very simplicity is a source of provocation to the adult world, and from this fact many of his gags derive. Again and again Harry's innocent, self-absorbed babyishness arouses anger in his fellow-men; and their anger, turned aside by his angel-guided guilelessness, springs back upon themselves.

His best moments are gentle, though: watching life and res-ponding to it with odd little twitches—acutely expressive of pleasure or distaste or sheer bewilderment—of his tiny Lillian Gish mouth; registering shock or disbelief with his wide baby eyes; or, in *Long Pants*, cycling foolishly round and round a car in which the adored one is sitting motionless, his pace slackening as in-fatuation mounts.

Harry Langdon, *Long Pants* 1927

Three other comics—a man and two girls—momentarily achieved the inspiration of these four giants. Raymond Griffith was a short, rather tubby young man who cultivated a moustache and an unvarying elegance that recalled Max Linder. He always proved serenely superior to the catastrophes he blandly evoked. In *Hands Up!* for instance he is a spy in the Civil War. Faced with a firing squad he diverts their aim by the devastatingly simple ruse of tossing plates into the air. Falling into the clutches of Indians, he

Raymond Griffith, *Changing Husbands*, 1924

first divests the Chief of his regalia in a fixed dice game, then persuades the tribe that the Charleston is a great improvement on their present war dance. Reputedly the best of his films, *Meet the Prince*, a satire on the tours of Edward, Prince of Wales, was never shown in this country. The coming of talking pictures had more significance for Griffith than for most comedians, since a serious and permanent throat affliction left him virtually voiceless.

Raymond Griffith, *Hands Up!*, 1926

Marion Davies, *Show People*, 1928

Marion Davies's extraordinary talents as a comedienne—particularly when she worked with a director of the stature of King Vidor —have been unjustly overshadowed by her celebrity as the friend of William Randolph Hearst. Her satire on the affectations and foibles of movie queens of the day in *Show People* is vigorous and sophisticated. It was a grave loss to the silent cinema that Beatrice Lillie made no more than one starring comedy, *Exit Smiling*. Brilliantly successful in adapting her unique comedy style to the visual needs of the cinema, she brought to the screen a comedy that was at once more sophisticated and more crazy than anything Hollywood had seen until that time. In this uniquely funny and attractive film, directed by Sam Taylor, she plays the maid-of-all-work in a touring repertory company, whose dreams of playing the *femme fatale* in the company's *pièce de résistance*, *Flaming Women*, are finally fulfilled one day when she is called upon to overwhelm a real-life villain (Harry Myers, later the alcoholic millionaire of *City Lights*) with her athletic line in vamping.

Beatrice Lillie and Harry Myers, *Exit Smiling*, 1926

# Death of an art

It is not sentimental nostalgia to claim that screen comedy never completely recovered from the arrival of talking pictures. Nor was the reason that there is anything specially sacred about silence: W. C. Fields and Laurel and Hardy, though they were successful in silent films, were only completely fulfilled when audiences heard their voices. The great comedians remained great; but the cinema changed, as industry and craft; and conditions were no longer ideal for comic creation as they had been in the era of silent cinema.

As films became bigger business, and pictures cost and made larger fortunes, the money men and bankers were attracted to Hollywood. Film-making was reorganized on the lines of large-scale industry. Many smaller companies were squeezed out in the amalgamations and consolidations of the 'twenties. The new men wanted to safeguard their investments by rationalizing production, by keeping to safe and known selling formulas, by eliminating uncertainties and unconventional production methods, by setting production supervisors over the artists and supervisors over the supervisors. A rare few, like Chaplin, were able to secure themselves independence in one way or another; but other comedians, like Langdon and Keaton, found that they had sacrificed their necessary independence, had become part of film factories which had neither time nor concern for the individualist. After 1929 Keaton never directed a film; and Langdon was only one of many stars who were toppled into obscurity.

Inevitably some comedians were disorientated by the fact of sound itself. They had unsuitable voices, or had brought their silent pantomime techniques to a refinement which they could not adjust to new technical demands. Film technique had lost the marvellous flexibility and freedom that had made possible the inventions of Sennett and the creative flights of the great clowns. For a start, sound films were much more complex and costly to make, and the free improvisation of many comedians, the high shooting ratios employed by others, terrified producers. Moreover, the sound cameras of the early days were huge and unwieldy. The cameramen could no longer freely follow the comedians' every whim and antic. Early sound films as a whole favoured artists who were prepared to stand where they were put and talk and talk and talk.

Perhaps the biggest loss to the comedian, however, was the potential of the sneak preview. All the great comics were accustomed to show their films at these unannounced previews, and subsequently to cut them or build up strong sequences or otherwise revise according to the lessons they learnt from the response of an unprejudiced audience. To the sneak preview must be credited a great deal of the polish and accuracy of the best silent comedy. Cutting sound film, however, is an elaborate and expensive business; and henceforward the comedians were obliged to forgo this creative collaboration of the audience's own reactions.

Finally, the coming of talking pictures brought to an end the internationalism which for three decades had been of equal cultural and economic benefit to the cinema. When audiences could no longer take for their own the comedians of other countries, and give them local names, the horizons of comedy narrowed.

## Laurel and Hardy, W. C. Fields

Happily there were comedians who successfully made the transition, apart from Chaplin who autocratically chose to ignore talking pictures for a decade or more. Charlie Chase and Will Rogers, as we have seen, only came into their own with talking pictures. The whiskery Scottish comedian, Andy Clyde, made a popular series for the oddly named Educational Film Company. A little later Edgar Kennedy and Leon Errol were to revive the art of the two-reel comedy. Kennedy (1890–1948) claimed to be the inventor of the 'slow burn', the technique of reacting a second or

Leon Errol, *Finn and Hattie*, 1931

Will Rogers, *A Connecticut Yankee*, 1931

two late to some shock or insult or indignity, thus at once prolonging the pleasure of the reaction and of the gag that produced it. Errol (1881–1951), with his bald head and tormented little face permanently twisted in discontent and anger, was Australian by birth and had enjoyed great success in the Follies and in musicals before making his first two-reeler in 1924. In the 'forties he acquired new popularity with the *Joe Palooka* series. Robert Benchley (1889–1945) was a writer and critic who turned to acting rather late in life, providing some memorable caricatures of upper middle-class and intellectual America.

The greatest comedy team which bridged the transition from silence to sound was Laurel and Hardy, a classic juxtaposition of thin and fat, the little man timid and afraid, the big one bullying and brash; and both of them magnificently foolish and incompetent. Laurel (1890–1965) came from Lancashire and arrived in the States, like Chaplin, with Fred Karno's music-hall company. Hardy (1892–1957) was from the deep Southern state of Georgia. Both had been around the Roach studios for years (and had even played in films together) before finally being teamed in 1927 for a beautifully ridiculous film called *Putting Pants on Philip*, which relates Oliver's embarrassment when Stanley arrives to visit him wearing a kilt. They are, Charles Barr has written, 'supreme liberators from bourgeois inhibition, yet essentially they are, or aspire to be, respectable bourgeois citizens'. Their very dress proclaims it—their bowlers and bow ties, their slightly rumpled suits, Stanley's strictly conservative, Oliver's slightly louder in cut. Their motives are (often) exemplary and they show due deference to authority and—at least in their presence—the virago wives which generally dog them. However rude and patronizing he is to Stanley, Ollie is unfailingly courteous and polite to policemen and strangers. But they are fated, by destiny as well as their own obtuseness. Inevitably they will bring about an orgy of destruction; and inevitably there will come a point when their bourgeois delight in propriety and order will break down and they will be released into ecstatic pleasure in chaos and destruction.

Their most violent and most characteristic piece of destruction occurs in *Big Business*. A trifling exchange of words with James Finlayson—their implacable enemy through countless film battles —over a Christmas tree which he prefers not to buy, leads to an

Laurel and Hardy with James Finlayson, *Big Business*, 1929
'A trifling exchange of words . . .

escalating contest of tit for tat, each party taking turns to inflict a worse vandalism upon the property of the other. Piece by piece, taking turns, with exquisite courtesy, Finlayson destroys their car while they wreck his house. When it is all over, and the whole neighbourhood reduced to tears, Laurel and Hardy suddenly leave off their crying to explode into incorrigible, shocking laughter.

At their best their films are variations on limited gag material. In *The Music Box* it takes all of two reels to get a piano up a flight of stairs and smash it up in the process. *County Hospital* is mostly concerned with the horrors of receiving a sick visit from Stanley. As they had survived the sound revolution, Laurel and Hardy moved into feature production with equal success. *Our Relations*, *Way Out West* and *Blockheads* are admirable. Only their last films —made with directors who were exhausted, like the once-great Mal St Clair, or who failed to understand their particular kind of comedy—showed a falling off. In their great period Stan Laurel had had the same kind of control over the conception, direction and editing of their films as Chaplin and Keaton demanded.

Laurel and Hardy with James Finlayson, *Big Business*, 1929
. . . an escalating contest'

W. C. Fields had appeared in silent films as early as 1915, with a success that was surprising in view of the essentially aural nature of much of his comedy. Improbably, he had played in two D. W. Griffith films, one of them a version of his own great stage success *Poppy*, in which he played Eustace McGargle, a fairground showman and confidence trickster—a character which was crucial to the shaping of his eventual comic persona. Fields was the most reprehensible clown ever to win the adoration of his audiences. He was mean, mendacious, larcenous, misanthropic and generally anti-social. He had thin hair, a huge and unlovely tippler's nose, eyes screwed up in dreadful suspicion, a thin, unyieldingly mean mouth. He professed to hate children and animals. He also hated—and portrayed in all their nasty colours—wives, sons, mothers-in-laws, daughters' fiancés, salesmen, bank-managers, policemen, film producers, motorists. He had a permanent air of watchfulness and a way of jerking up his elbows if addressed suddenly, either in self-defence or simply to secure his hat. His unoiled creak of a voice was always ready to turn from whining complaint to sly untruth, shameless braggadaccio or uniquely angry yelps of pain.

In private life Fields—a rather solitary and mysterious man of unpredictable turns of cruelty and sentimentality—cultivated a character not unlike the people he played on the screen; and it was possibly the mixture of guile, pleading, bullying and treachery that gave him sufficient independence, in most of the group of films he made in the 'thirties (he generally wrote his own stories, and his brilliant ad-libbing was the despair of orderly-minded directors), to impose one of the strongest, strangest and most distinctive personalities in the history of comedy.

## The 'thirties

The coming of sound saw in general a renewed recruitment of talent from vaudeville and musical comedy. At the same time the great craze for radio had introduced a new kind of comedy and comedian whose appeal was principally aural. The early radio stars attained enormous celebrity and were inevitably brought to Hollywood. Only one of them, Jack Benny, was able to sustain his success in films, thanks to his wry underplaying and his very consistent character creation as 'the meanest man on earth'. He made a marvellously prissy *Charley's American Aunt*, though his greatest comedy success was perhaps in Lubitsch's *To Be Or Not To Be*. One of Benny's regular radio partners, the excellent Negro comedian 'Rochester' Anderson, also appeared in films with him. Unhappily the fear of Uncle Tom-ism limited the later activity of several excellent Negro comedians—Stepin Fetchit, Willie Best, Butterfly McQueen—who also appeared in the 'thirties.

Jack Benny, *Charley's American Aunt*, 1941

Eddie 'Rochester' Anderson, *c.* 1938

Joe E. Brown, *Fireman, Save My Child!*, 1932

*Opposite*
Eddie Cantor, *c.* 1932

Of the recruits from musical comedy, the Jewish comedian Eddie Cantor enjoyed an immense vogue throughout most of the 'thirties, with his popping eyes, his polished song-and-dance routines and his breathless, vital comedy. Joe E. Brown had begun his career at nine years old in a vaudeville acrobatic act; and just as his face with its great comic mouth and gentle eyes seemed a traditional clown mask, his comic style always looked back to an

100

older circus and music hall tradition. Jimmie ('Schnozzle') Durante, too, with his notable features and gravel voice, has always recalled the great days of vaudeville. Wheeler and Woolsey were first recruited to the cinema when they came to Hollywood in 1929 to recreate their original stage roles in *Rio Rita*. Among these musical comedy talents brought to the screen in the 'thirties, Bob Hope has been unique in sustaining his career with unbroken success into the 'sixties. A comedian of great style, his character is based on a self-confidence that is always being assaulted but never diminished. His first big success came with the *Road to . . .* series of films in which he co-starred with Bing Crosby and the witty Dorothy Lamour; and his career received new impetus with *Paleface* and *Son of Paleface*, the second of which was directed by the redoubtable clown-maker Frank Tashlin.

*Opposite*
Lucille Ball and Bob Hope, *Fancy Pants*, 1950

Jimmy Durante, *You're In the Army Now*, 1941

In *Fancy Pants* Hope found an ideal partner in Lucille Ball, a true lady clown of great beauty and wit who, like Hope, has managed to sustain her popularity, with only temporary setbacks, for well over thirty years. She made her first film appearance in the Eddie Cantor vehicle *Roman Scandals*; and in recent years has enjoyed international popularity with various television series which she has herself produced. Other lady comics who began their screen careers in the 'thirties were Martha Raye, with her enormous mouth and predatory habits, and Elsa Lanchester, the English wife of the English actor, Charles Laughton. Most spectacular, however, was Mae West, whose insolent parodies of the American way of sex invigorated the cinema until the Hays Office began to comprehend the triple meanings of her *doubles entendres*.

*On pages 104 and 105*
Chico and Harpo Marx with Margaret Dumont, *Animal Crackers*, 1930

*Opposite*
Mae West, *I'm No Angel*, 1933

Martha Raye and Jimmy Durante, *Billy Rose's Jumbo*, 1962

In the natural course of artistic diffusion, the dada and surrealist impulses had by the 'thirties reached the level of popular art; which perhaps to an extent explains the vogue for a crazy or zany or surrealist style in comedy. The pioneers of the type were of course the Marx Brothers, a family troupe of Jewish comedians who were brought to Hollywood after the success of their musical shows in New York in the late 'twenties. In so far as their method can be defined, it is a comedy of insult; and Groucho has claimed that the secret of their appeal was that the audience would itself like to provoke and insult people as he and Chico do, or to chase girls with the obscene abandon of Harpo, the non-articulate brother. None of the crazy teams which followed them—notably the Ritz Brothers and The Three Stooges—had either the Marx's professional polish (the outcome of painstaking preparation which went into every one of their films) or their sustained success. The

Zeppo and Groucho Marx with Margaret Dumont, *Duck Soup*, 1933

same taste for crazy comedy brought to the screen Olsen and Johnson's long-running stage success *Hellzapoppin'*. A sentimental story was hung about with inconsequential, often surreal humour which, as recent viewings have proved, still looks fresh after almost thirty years.

Among the incidental pleasures of *Hellzapoppin'*, apart from the stars and Martha Raye, were Mischa Auer and F. Hugh

Mischa Auer, Ole Olsen and Chick Johnson, *Hellzapoppin'*, 1941

W. C. Fields and Franklin Pangborne, *The Bank Dick*, 1940

Herbert, who are representative of the wealth of supporting character comedians whom Hollywood produced in this period. Jack Norton was the greatest of all comic drunks. Sissy Franklin Pangborne, generally the victim of W. C. Fields' treacheries, was around as early as the Beatrice Lillie *Exit Smiling*. Among the rest were the ever-distressed and stammering Edward Everett Horton; Eric Blore and Ernest Essent, the eternal butlers; Allen Jenkins, Edward Brophy, Eugene Pallette, William Frawley, S. Z. Sakall, Guy Kibbee, and marvellous ladies like the virago Minerva Urecal, Hope Emerson, Almira Sessions and Margaret Hamilton, the wicked witch to Billie Burke's dotty good one in *The Wizard of Oz*. There were dizzy girls like Vera Vague, Mary Wickes and Una Merkel; and incorrigibly lady-like ones such as Florence Bates and the statuesque Margaret Dumont who was forever exposed to the insulting attentions of Groucho Marx. (W. C. Fields had his turn with her too in *Never Give a Sucker an Even Break*.)

## Britain and France

The British music hall had enriched the cinema of the whole world apart from Britain. In the earliest days Little Tich and Harry Fragson had been a powerful influence upon the development of French comedy; and the two Chaplins, Stan Laurel, Lupino Lane, Jimmy Aubrey, Billy Armstrong, Albert Austin, Billy Reeves and

The Crazy Gang (Allen, Gold, Nervo, Flanagan, Knox, Naughton), *Alf's Button Afloat*, 1938

Gracie Fields, Frank Pettingell and Duggie Wakefield, *This Week of Grace*, 1933

James Finlayson were all emigrants from the English halls to the American screen. As it happened, not until the 'thirties when the live music hall tradition was already fast dying, did variety make a notable contribution to the British cinema. A number of music hall acts turned to the screen. An entirely native equivalent to the Marx Brothers, the Crazy Gang were already a highly popular knockabout troupe of verve and vulgarity on the stage before they were launched in a series of lively low-budget pictures. Gracie Fields' characterizations of the Northern working classes had an enormous appeal in a cinema which had otherwise not generally favoured a regional culture. George Formby too had a considerable vogue with comedies in which he played a Northern simpleton, a fresh and attractive updating of the character his father had created on the Edwardian music halls. The lugubrious Sydney Howard, with his devastatingly solemn delivery of lines of the wildest absurdity is one of the most unjustly neglected comedians of this period. Other music-hall artists who enjoyed brief but spectacular success in the 'thirties and 'forties were Tommy Trinder and Sid Field. Two comedians who had made

Sydney Howard, *Fame*, 1936

George Formby, *Come on George*, 1939

their names on British radio, even though their careers were deeply rooted in the music hall, were Arthur Askey, a genuine clown, tiny, large-headed, with his characteristic 'mask' of a huge smile and horn-rimmed glasses; and Tommy Handley, who made a few films during the early war period on the strength of the enormous popularity of his radio series *It's That Man Again*.

*Opposite*
Arthur Askey, *Band Wagon*, 1940

Tommy Handley, *Time Flies*, 1944

The most original and enduring film comedian produced in Britain in the 'thirties was Will Hay. He did not look like a comedian. He had a plain, ordinary, cross sort of face, a marked speech defect and a regular air of puzzled irritation. He always personified figures of authority—schoolmasters, policemen, station masters, prison governors—to whom he imparted an air of seediness and corruption. If he was not beset by a school of unruly and generally rather aged boys, he was teamed with Moore Marriott and Graham Moffatt, respectively a capering, sly ,whiskery, senile old idiot and a gross and idle youth of Dickensian mould.

Will Hay with Claude Hulbert, *The Ghost of St Michael's*, 1941

From the musical comedy stage British films derived Jack Hulbert and Cicely Courtneidge—he suave and cool; she agressively vital and given to funny clothes—and Hulbert's amiably idiot brother Claude. The Aldwych farces, whose regular players included Tom Walls, Alfred Drayton, Robertson Hare and Gordon Harker, were regularly transferred to the screen with little artistic flair but enormous popular success.

Cicely Courtneidge and Jack Hulbert, *Jack's the Boy*, 1932

Towards the end of the 'thirties there was a considerable output of films intended primarily for the (supposedly) less sophisticated north-country market—so regional did British culture remain in pre-television days. Made on minimal budgets, these films starred a group of comedians of rich vulgarity and great talent. Norman Evans, a rubber-faced Lancastrian, specialized in outrageous caricatures of busty north-country house-wives. Frank Randle did beautiful drunk and senile impersonations, often working with a team of positively mediaeval grotesques, including the admirable, lanky, rubber-limbed Nat Jackley. Best of all was Arthur Lucan whose Old Mother Riley was at once vulgar, comic, touching and true to working-class life. Old Mother Riley was a belligerent, kindly washerwoman whose life revolved around her gin, her corsets and her lovely daughter Kitty—played until a dangerously advanced age by Lucan's wife Kitty McShane.

*Opposite*
Fernandel, *Le Rosier de Madame Husson*, 1932

Arthur Lucan, *Old Mother Riley, M.P.*, 1939

Noël-Noël, *Les Carnets de Major Thompson*, 1955

*Opposite*
Toto, *L'Imperatore de Capri*, 1950

The French music hall gave the cinema one of its most durable comic stars, the horse-faced Fernandel, who had worked in his youth with Dranem (see page 16) and whose career as a star comedian has been unbroken since his first film appearance in 1930. Both Bach and Noël-Noël were popular *chansonniers* before their successes in films in the 'thirties—Noël-Noël specializing in excellent personifications of French bourgeois life. France's greatest comic performer, Michel Simon, is too versatile an actor to be typed simply as a clown. The prodigious talent which has always triumphed over his extraordinary physical appearance—in his youth he was constantly advised that an acting career was impossible for anyone so ugly—gives to his funniest performances (in Renoir's *Tire au flanc* or *Boudu sauvé des eaux*, for instance), an undertone of seriousness and sometimes tragedy.

George Voscovec and Jan Werich, *Hej Rup!*, 1934

## Since the war

The war and post-war cinemas saw the emergence of many new comedians in America and Europe; but without the necessary perspective of time it is hard to predict which if any of them will, in the sight of history, prove the equal of the classic clowns, of Linder, Keaton, Lloyd or Fields. If they do not, the fault will not necessarily lie in the artists: the times do not so easily accommodate giants as did the 'twenties and early 'thirties. Among the most successful comics of the 'forties were Abbott and Costello. Today it is hard to understand their success. They indulged in broad slapstick and

Bud Abbott and Lou Costello, *Jack and the Beanstalk*, 1952

Red Skelton, *Whistling in Brooklyn*, 1943

*Opposite*
Danny Kaye, *On the Double*, 1961

crude parodies of popular *genres*. Costello's flabby infantilism was a far cry from the genial babyishness of Langdon or Laurel. Danny Kaye emerged in the early 'forties as a comedian of accomplishment, but perhaps, like Red Skelton, who came to stardom slightly earlier, of an over-calculated *genre* of humour. The charm of Donald O'Connor lay more in his bright personality than in his comic ability. His appearance in the unfortunate *Buster Keaton Story* was a serious error of judgement. A more authentic clown

126

figure who made his name in the same period is Phil Silvers, a sort of disreputable Harold Lloyd, a horn-rimmed hustler whose methods are usually as reprehensible as his motives. The lamented

Judy Holliday with Frank Gorshin, *Bells Are Ringing*, 1960

Judy Holliday came from the stage in the 'forties to be one of the screen's most touching dizzy blondes, with a blank simplicity that was from time to time illuminated by disconcerting insights.

Marilyn Monroe and Tom Ewell, *The Seven Year Itch*, 1955

Jack Lemmon and Walter Matthau, *The Odd Couple*, 1968

The 'fifties saw the emergence of Jack Lemmon and the occasional screen appearance of the excellent stage comic Tom Ewell; recognition of the immense comedy potential of Hermione Gingold; and several notable additions to the roster of supporting players, including John McIver and Peter Falk, Tony Curtis's squint-eyed familiar in *The Great Race*.

Hermione Gingold, *The Music Man*, 1962

The truly original comic talent in contemporary American films, however, is Jerry Lewis. His very extraordinary personality, the extravagance with which he contorts his physique—body, face and voice—in the service of his comedy, were not fully realized until he was directed by Frank Tashlin in the later films of his partnership with Dean Martin. Tashlin, who originally worked as a maker of animated films, has brought to comedy something of the surrealist violence and nonsense logic of cartoons; and the style seemed to bring out the best qualities in Jerry Lewis. Jerry is essentially an adolescent, with an adolescent's physical and social awkwardness, and motivated by an adolescent's sexual and career daydreams. In the more recent films which he has directed himself, Lewis had attempted with intermittent success (for his invention is spasmodic and his performance often lacking in a sense of comic rhythm) to formularize a revived slapstick comedy.

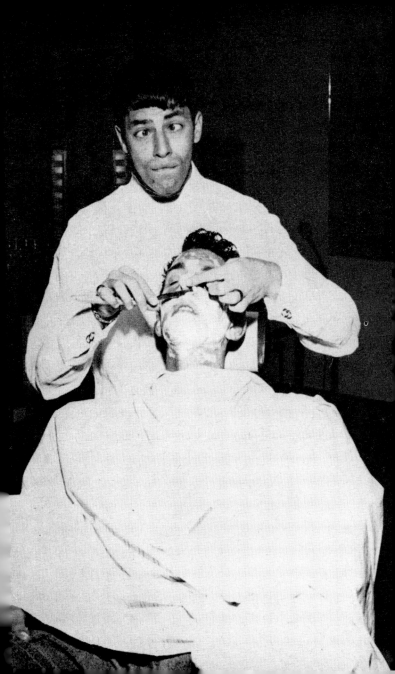

The most important post-war revival of comedy in Britain was the series of films made at Ealing Studios in the early 'fifties, which exploited the great comic talents of such legitimate stage players as Alec Guinness and Alastair Sim (who had appeared with the Crazy Gang in the 'thirties). In the wake of Ealing comedy came a new appreciation of British character players, most notably the excellent Margaret Rutherford, who had been in films since the 'thirties but who only achieved star status in the 'fifties and 'sixties.

Margaret Rutherford, *Murder She Said*, 1961

Ian Carmichael and Peter Sellers, *Heavens Above*, 1963

*Opposite*
Norman Wisdom and Jerry Desmonde, *Trouble in Store*, 1953

Television, which in the 'fifties seemed to have assumed the former role of the music hall, by this time on the point of extinction, offered new stars. Norman Wisdom's earliest appearances on television and in the film *Trouble in Store* (in which, as in later films, he worked with the great comic 'feed' Jerry Desmonde) promised a clown in the great tradition; but poor material and worse judgement frustrated the hope. Peter Sellers, less a clown

Terry-Thomas with Richard Beymer, *Bachelor Flat*, 1961

than a protean comic actor, and Terry-Thomas whose seedy swells
have a touch of Linder in them, have both achieved international
reputation. Jimmy Edwards, Charlie Drake, Morecambe and Wise
and Spike Milligan have all been thrust into films which have made
little attempt to exploit their potential comic gifts. Two of the
finest television comedians, Arthur Haynes and Tony Hancock,
each of whom possessed an authentic and original comic vision
of the new working-class of the 'sixties, both died before their full
possibilities could be realized in the cinema.

Jimmy Edwards, *Bottoms Up*, 1959

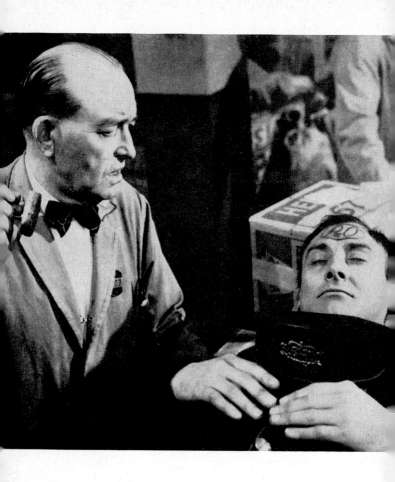

Spike Milligan, *Postman's Knock*, 1961
140

Charlie Drake, *Petticoat Pirates*, 1961

Charles Hawtrey, Phil Silvers, Kenneth Williams, *Follow That Camel*, 1968

*Opposite*
Cantinflas, *Around the World in Eighty Days*, 1956

The *Carry On* series and its various relatives and imitators exploits a crudely contrived and unpolished vein of low comedy, but exerts a certain charm by reason of the familiarity of the regular character players who appear in them—Sidney James, Charles Hawtrey (a one-time Will Hay schoolboy), Kenneth Williams, Hattie Jaques, Joan Sims, Liz Fraser and Jim Dale, a sweet natural whose appearances as Shakespearean clown have shown his clear continuity with antique traditions of bucolic foolery.

In a period of co-productions clowning has again acquired a degree of internationalism. The Mexican comedian Cantinflas enchanted European audiences in *Around the World in Eighty Days*.

Giulietta Massina, *Luci del Varietà*, 1950

The melancholy Italian Alberto Sordi has become familiar to American and British audiences, though of his countrymen, Renato Rascel is mainly known in Britain for his theatrical appearances, while comics of the calibre of Macario, Taranto, Chiari and even the great Toto—a lean, unsmiling, irresistibly comical man who came from variety and operetta and was in private life Prince Antonio di Bizancio—remain unknown outside Italy. Giulietta Massina, the wife of Federico Fellini with whom she has done her most important film work, is perhaps Italy's first lady clown.

Apart from the star of *Seventeen*, Ole Soltoft, whose deft and unassuming light comedy is readily accessible, Scandinavian comedians—Sweden's Nils Poppe, Denmark's Madsen and Schenstrom,

Leonid Kharitonov and Dae Smirnova, *Private Ivan Brovkin*, 1956

Jensen and Lauritzen Sr—have remained practically unknown outside their own countries. Nor have the Eastern European states produced identifiable schools of comedy, excepting the recent films of the new Prague school of film-makers which discover the unbroken vein of comedy that lies just below the surfaces of every-day life and everyday people ;* and occasional glimpses of a black, anarchic humour in Polish films like *Eve Wants to Sleep* and Andrzej Munk's *Bad Luck*, with its excellent comic actor Bogumit Kobiela. The Soviet Union has a thin record in comedy. In the 'fifties a pleasant young comic, Leonid Kharitonov, enjoyed national popularity with two films about the adventures of a myth-ically incompetent soldier, *Private Ivan Brovkin*. More recently

* In 1934 the distinguished Czech stage actors Voscovec and Werich turned expert clowning to the service of social satire in *Hej Rup!*

Bogumit Kobiela, *Bad Luck*, 1960

Robert Dhéry, Louis de Funes, *La Belle Americaine*, 1961

Bourvil, Terry-Thomas, Louis de Fünes, *Les Grandes Vadrouilles*, 1966

Yuri Nikulin, the principal comedian in *Operation Laughter*, has revealed a sturdy peasant comedy, while Innokenti Smoktunovsky, the Soviet film Hamlet, showed an unexpected flair for poker-face clowning in *Beware, Automobile!*

Once again, however, it seems that the comic initiative has passed back to France, which has produced some of the most original and promising comedians of the past twenty years, among them Robert Dhéry and the members of his company, Louis de Fünes, with his disconcerting facial twitches, Francis Blanche, Jean-Pierre Cassell and Bourvil, who can turn with surprising versatility from slow-witted peasant roles to that of the phoney priest who lives by robbing poor boxes, in *Drôle de Paroissien*.

With grave deliberation Pierre Etaix, who began his professional career as a circus clown, has endeavoured to revive in the cinema the classic mime, with some quality of the old silent film comedies. He is small, solemn, neat and handsome; his invention is prolific; his comedy stylish. His features, *Le Soupirant, Yoyo* and *Tant qu'on a la santé* all leave a sense of frustration. Perhaps it is the romanticism which tends to a too fey quality; or a sense of self-conscious revivalism and the recognition that the silent comedy (which is Etaix's aim) is ultimately an anachronism. There is still no question of his real originality and value.

Pierre Etaix, *Le Soupirant*, 1962

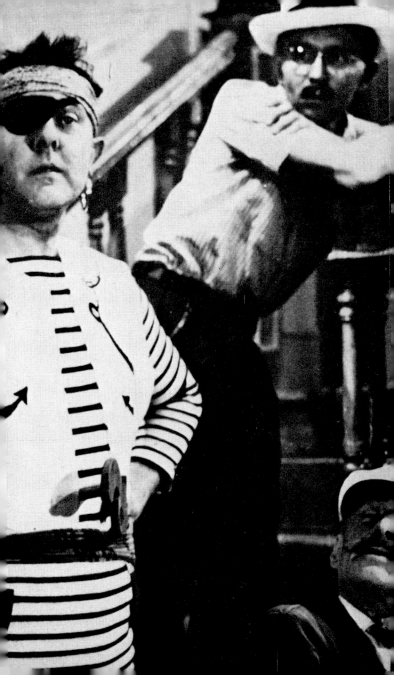

Nor can there be any doubt that Jacques Tati is one of the very great comic creators of the cinema. He is himself droll, with his loping walk, his shapeless hat, raincoat, too-short trousers, suede bootees, his invariable pipe and the umbrella which seems to have a life of its own and is always mildly teasing him in some way or other. But Tati creates a whole comic universe around his Monsieur Hulot. Viewed through the eyes of Hulot-Tati the world of the 'fifties and 'sixties is incorrigibly, inescapably comical. 'Ce que j'ai essayé . . . c'est de prouver et faire voir que, dans le fond, tout le monde était amusant.' The little village community of *Jour de Fête*, the seaside resort of *Les Vacances de Monsieur Hulot*, the automated factory and house of *Mon Oncle*, the whole brave new steel and plastic Paris of *Playtime*, with its shops and offices and restaurants—every chair and door and car and telephone in them—are all jokes. It is a wonderland in which Tati lovingly, cruelly, indulgently, uncomprehendingly watches the antics of the people who have made their world and now scuttle about in it with the pride of White Rabbits. Tati's view of the universe is unique in the history of film comedy, for it leaves us all with the conviction that all men were made in clown's image.

*On pages 152 and 153*
Jacques Tati, *Les Vacances de Monsieur Hulot* ,1952

Jacques Tati, *Playtime*, 1968
154

155

The clowns will keep on coming as long as there are people. (What of Ringo and Robert Morse and Doris Day who has become a new Margaret Dumont?) Their metier is demanding, hard and even dangerous. Keaton broke his ankle and his neck and nearly drowned in the pursuit of his film-making. Lloyd lost a couple of fingers and the sight of one eye. Ultimately it was the too great burden of their calling that took the lives of Linder, Normand, Semon, and perhaps Hancock and others too. But the clowns understand that their work, though often painful and sometimes tragic, is vital to society: the distorting mirrors they hold up to nature often return surprisingly revealing images of our true selves.

Pierre Etaix, *Tant qu'on a la santé*, 1968

# Index

*Page numbers not in italics refer to text references*

22-100

T 913